KILLERTON HOUSE

Devon

THE NATIONAL TRUST

Acknowledgements

The National Trust is happy to reiterate Lady Acland's thanks to the many friends and neighbours who helped her with their personal memories of Killerton in days gone. It is also grateful to Laetitia Erbes, Keith Melhuish (for the bird's-eye view) and all the staff at Devon Record Office in Exeter.

Sources and Further Reading

Some of the Acland Papers are in the Devon Record Office in Exeter. James Wyatt's drawings for the unbuilt house were presented to the RIBA by Lady Acland in 1969.

ACKERMANN, Rudolph, *The Repository of Arts*, London, 1828, xi, pl. 25; ACLAND, Anne, *A Devon Family*, Chichester, 1981; BRIGGS, Nancy, 'Woolvestone Hall: Some Reflections on the Domestic Architecture of John Johnson (1732–1814)', *Proceedings of the Suffolk Institute of Archaeology and History*, xxxiv, part 1, 1977; BRITTON, J., and E. W. BRAYLEY, *Devonshire Illustrated*, London, 1829, pp. 34–5; FULLER, K. A. P, and J. M. LANGDON, 'The House of Veitch', *International Dendrology Society Year Book*, 1882; LACEY, Stephen, *Gardens of the National Trust*, London, 1996, pp. 154–7; LAMBERT, Anthony, *Devon from old photographs*, London, 1993; LE FANU HUGHES, Penelope, '"One of your best Pupils": Francis Nicholson and the Hon. Henrietta Ann Fortescue', *Old Water-Colour Society Club*, lxiii, 1994; LOCKE, Geoffrey, 'Ice Houses', *National Trust Magazine*, Autumn 1975; MELLER, Hugh, 'Harriet, Lady Acland, on the River Hudson', *Apollo*, April 1993, p. 273; SALES, John, 'Rites of Spring', *Country Life*, 23 February 1995, pp. 58–63; WATKIN, David, *C. R. Cockerell*, London, 1974 [drawings for the chapel in the RIBA]; WILCOX, Timothy, *Francis Towne*, Tate Gallery, London, 1997, pp. 131–2.

Photographs: National Trust pp. 33, 40 (bottom); National Trust/Nicholas Toyne pp. 4, 31, 46, 47; NT/Chris Vile pp. 5, 23, 24, 44, back cover; National Trust Photographic Library front cover, p. 22; NTPL/Andrew Butler pp. 6, 26, 28, 29, 30, 36; NTPL/Andreas von Einsiedel p. 21 (bottom); NTPL/David Garner pp. 7, 10, 14, 16, 18; NTPL/Dennis Gilbert pp. 1, 13, 20, 21 (top), 41, 42, 43; NTPL/John Hammond pp. 8, 9, 15, 17, 34 (top and bottom), 35, 37, 38, 39, 40 (top), 48; NTPL/Chris King p. 32.

Birds-eye view by Keith Melhuish

Registered charity no. 205846

ISBN 1-84359-120-0

Reprinted 2004; revised 2005

Typeset from disc and designed by James Shurmer

Print managed by Astron
for the National Trust (Enterprises) Ltd,
36 Queen Anne's Gate, London SW1H 9AS

(*Front cover*) Killerton in 1818; engraving by D. Havell

(*Title-page*) A view of Killerton appears on this Crown Derby vase, *c.*1830, in the Music Room

(*Back cover*) The Terrace borders

CONTENTS

KILLERTON HOUSE

Killerton House is the focal point of a substantial agricultural estate of 2,585 hectares (6,399 acres), given to the National Trust in 1944 by Sir Richard Acland. The Aclands (probably the oldest family in Devon to claim a direct descent in the male line) settled in this part of the country in the sixteenth century and earned the hereditary title of baronet by their loyalty to the King in the Civil War. The present house was built in 1778–9 by Sir Thomas Dyke Acland, 7th Baronet (1722–85), to the design of John Johnson, and was first intended simply as a temporary residence while something grander was being built on the hill behind. In the event, Johnson's house was allowed to stand, though it has since been much altered to suit the needs of an intensely active family which has never been afraid of change. It is not a showpiece in the accepted sense, but it nevertheless has a special appeal for visitors, who are often heard to declare that they 'can imagine living here' more easily than in greater and more stately homes.

The real glory of Killerton is the garden, first planted when the house was built, and only once neglected since. Famous for its rare trees and shrubs – rhododendrons in particular – it gains greatly from its splendid setting below Dolbury Hill ('the Clump'), 'the pride of Killerton and ornament of this part of the country', as an early topographer described it, with a 'fine panoramic prospect over a great extent of highly cultivated and varied landscape'. Spring is the most spectacular season, but there is no day in the year when you cannot find something of interest and beauty in Killerton Garden. The active can climb to the top of the Clump and enjoy wide views on every side; you will meet few other people to disturb your peace.

(Left) Sir Francis Acland, 14th Bt, playing 'Bumble Puppy', a family version of skittles, in the 1930s

(Right) The Coade stone urns contrast with the informal planting of the Terrace borders

TOUR OF THE HOUSE

The Exterior

Killerton House was rebuilt in 1778–9 by Sir Thomas Acland, 7th Bt, who told his architect, John Johnson, to design a 'temporary residence'. In the end, the house became a permanency. Extra rooms had to be added to suit the needs of later generations and it is a series of these extensions which visitors first see when they approach Killerton today. The most recent is the entrance porch, built in 1924 by Sir Francis Acland, 14th Bt; the architect was Randall Wells (1877–1942), and the arched doorway – a background for many family snapshots in the 1920s and '30s – is typical of his style. The projecting single-storey wing on the north side of the porch was built as a billiard room and study by Sir Charles Acland, 12th Bt, as part of an ambitious scheme of alterations which he carried out with the Cheltenham firm of architects, Protheroe and Phillips. This room is now used by the National Trust for conferences and exhibitions.

On the other side of the porch is a large projecting window bay which was added by Sir Thomas Acland, 10th Bt (the 'Great Sir Thomas'), in the 1820s, when Killerton was full to overflowing with his family and friends. To complete the confusion of periods on this side of the house, there is a stone from an earlier building bearing the date 1680, below a window-sill on the narrow projecting bay near the garden door.

The modest house which Johnson originally designed can best be seen from the terrace on the south front. It is very plain: the only remarkable feature is the fine recessed doorway (the 'Frontispiece' as the stonemason termed it), which was a notable item in the building accounts. The ships' cannon on the forecourt come from a family yacht, *The Lady of St Kilda*, in which the Great Sir Thomas and his wife Lydia made many intrepid voyages in the 1830s. The guns were last fired to celebrate the

double victory of Sir Francis and his son Richard at the General Election of 1935.

The marvellous view of the garden, which opens up round the corner of the house, also reveals the extent to which the building was enlarged in the early nineteenth century. As the Great Sir Thomas's family grew in number, he added more and more rooms and connected them to the garden with an elegant system of balconies: the first-floor nurseries at the far end were level with the ground, and children could run straight out – perhaps to picnic in the Bear's Hut, where tea-things and firewood were always kept ready. The first-floor rooms at this end of the house are now used by the National Trust as its Devon Regional Office. The link between the house and its setting, which has always been Killerton's special charm, was further emphasised by the terrace and herbaceous border, which were made by Sir Charles and Lady Acland in 1905 on the advice of the famous gardener William Robinson. The two handsome urns in the border path came from Mrs Eleanor Coade's celebrated artificial stone manufactory at Lambeth. They are impressed with the date 1805. The semicircular embrasure, from which Lloyd George once addressed 19,000 people in the park, makes an excellent place to sit and enjoy the view of the garden before exploring it in detail.

The Interior

THE ENTRANCE HALL

This is the newest part of the house, built by Sir Francis Acland in 1924 after a destructive fire. Eleanor, Lady Acland described the scene in a letter to her son: 'There was such a roar of flame we thought the whole house would go. Poor old Killerton! It is sad to stand in the kitchen and look up at black rafters and sky.' The architect Randall Wells was asked to design a hall with plenty of space for the comings and goings of a large, hospitable family. It never stayed tidy for long: the large central table, neatly arranged every morning with folded newspapers and a choice of two fresh buttonholes for Sir Francis, was usually littered with mackintoshes, fishing rods, maps and torn

(Left)
The entrance front. The original 1778–9 house is on the left; the single-storey wing on the right was added in 1900, and the porch in 1924

(Right)
The Entrance Hall was added in 1924 after a fire

envelopes by the end of the day. The broad window seat was a good place to read one's letters on a sunny morning.

PICTURES

OPPOSITE FRONT DOOR:

Sir Richard Acland, 15th Bt (1906–90), the donor of Killerton to the National Trust, by Bernard Dunstan (b. 1920), 1977.

ALONG WALL TO RIGHT:

Engraved portraits of members of the Acland family and their friends. Six of these are by Samuel Cousins (1801–87), who was born in Exeter. Agnes Acland, granddaughter of the Great Sir Thomas, explained how these came to be at Killerton: 'Grandfather helped Samuel Cousins in boyhood, and in gratitude SC sent some of his most beautiful engravings to Killerton … Mr Cousins was thin and as stiff as though a ramrod were down his back, and quaintly old fashioned.'

LEFT OF DOOR TO STUDY:

Charcoal drawing of the head of a dog, by Samuel Cousins aged ten.

LEFT OF MUSIC ROOM DOOR:

Two landscapes in watercolour; one by Henrietta, wife of the 9th Baronet. Other examples of work by members of the family are displayed throughout the

This drawing was made in 1811 by Samuel Cousins, who was then a ten-year-old charity boy at the Bluecoat School in Exeter. Thanks to the support of the Acland family, he went on to have a successful career as an artist

house, notably in the panelled passage between the Entrance Hall and the Staircase Hall. These include views of Killerton by Sir Thomas Acland, 10th Bt, and a drawing of Broadclyst by Anne, Lady Acland, wife of the 15th Baronet.

SCULPTURE

RIGHT OF MUSIC ROOM DOOR:

Bust of the Great Sir Thomas by the Devon sculptor Edward Bowring Stephens (1815–82), who also carved the 1861 statue of Sir Thomas in Northenhay Gardens, Exeter.

Turn right into the Study.

THE STUDY

This room, leading off the Entrance Hall, was built in 1900 as part of the alterations to Killerton carried out by Sir Charles Thomas Dyke Acland, 12th Bt. It was intended as a billiard room (at that time the favourite fashionable addition to a country house), with extra space allowed for a 'bookshelf part or study'. The architect Henry Protheroe (1848–1906) was scholarly, conscientious and not afraid to stand up to his client. Sometimes this was too much for Sir Charles, who was used to having his own way. On one occasion he wrote to his architect 'begging' to say that 'while allowing that differences of opinion must exist on matters of taste … they ought to be expressed *occasionally* and with proper temper'. Protheroe was unabashed and continued in his efforts to produce a new room worthy of the old Killerton.

The best feature is probably the ceiling. The ornamental plasterwork was carried out by a firm which still exists, Messrs Jackson of London. They used moulds (which are still preserved) made from original designs by the Adam brothers, and the work is delicate. The classical figures in the four oval panels, however, are hard to identify.

Sir Charles was keen to panel the whole room with cedarwood from the Holnicote estate, but (to the relief of Protheroe) not enough was available. He restricted its use to the doors, and directed that the walls should be 'practically white'. A suitable period mantelpiece was specially bought in

London, but this has now been moved to the Dining Room and replaced with another by the National Trust.

A door at the furthest end of the room leads directly to what used to be called 'The Steward's Entrance'. Through this door, the agent, farm tenants or estate workmen could come to discuss their problems with Sir Charles without disturbing the rest of the house.

It is not clear how much the room was ever used for billiards. Eventually, the table went to another part of the house and the room became known only as the Study. After 'Uncle Charlie's' death in 1919, a more light-hearted generation took it over for carpentry, wood-turning and boat-building, keeping their sporting guns on the bookshelves and a dart-board on the door. The pockmarks in the panelling could be seen until recently. The room was redecorated most recently in 2003. Today the Study is often used for temporary exhibitions.

PICTURES

The pictures are all connected with Grillion's Club, a London dining club founded in 1813 by the Great Sir Thomas and a few of his friends with the object of bringing together men of differing political

Sir Thomas Dyke Acland commissioned portraits of the members of Grillion's Club, which he had helped to found in 1813

9

opinions. Whigs and Tories, who had been roundly abusing one another in Parliament, would sit to dine in the greatest good humour at Grillion's Hotel in Albermarle Street on alternate Wednesdays during the session. Sir Thomas commissioned portrait drawings of every member from the artists Joseph Slater and George Richmond, and engravings of these (shown here) adorned the room where the club dined.

ABOVE STEWARD'S ENTRANCE:

Sir Charles Acland, a chalk drawing of 1900 by Henry Wells (1828–1903).

ON THE WEST WALL:

Sir Thomas Dyke Acland, 11th Bt (1809–98) by Cyril Johnson.

Mary, Lady Acland (d. 1892), the second wife of the 11th Baronet, painted in 1883 by Cyril Johnson.

THE MUSIC ROOM

This was the dining room when the house was rebuilt in 1778–9. Forty years later, the Great Sir Thomas enlarged it by adding a deep window bay and the scagliola columns with Ionic capitals at the opposite end. The room takes its name from the chamber organ, which was built by William Gray in 1807 for Sir Thomas's bride-to-be, Lydia Hoare. She took lessons from Samuel Sebastian Wesley, the organist of Exeter Cathedral, who 'respectfully dedicated' to Lady Acland his *Six Pieces for Chamber Organ*, written for this instrument. It was rebuilt later, to the detriment of its original character.

In the days of Sir Francis, in the 1920s and '30s, the Music Room became the heart of the household. Here, everybody would gather after breakfast to make plans for the day, sit round the fire at tea-time, and assemble after dinner to hear Sir Francis's wife, Eleanor, sing and play the piano. An unfinished (home-made) jigsaw puzzle was kept on

The Music Room

one table, and the sofa generally held one or two dogs, despite vain attempts to dislodge them by the master of the house. Music, reading, political argument and intimate conversation all went on in the Music Room, regardless of the continual traffic on the staircase. Sir Francis would sit writing at his table, undisturbed by all the din.

The fireplace is Italian, made in the 1840s for nearby Silverton Park and moved to Killerton following the demolition of that house in 1900.

PICTURES

OVER FIREPLACE:

Lydia, Lady Acland (1786–1856), wife of the Great Sir Thomas, with their two eldest sons, Tom, aged five, and Arthur, aged three, and their spaniel, Bronte. They were painted in 1814–15 by Sir Thomas Lawrence to celebrate Lydia's recovery from an illness. At that time, young boys wore skirts until they were 'breeched' at six or seven. The background shows the Exe valley beyond Killerton Clump. The picture was bought by the National Trust with the help of the Miss M. R. N. Harmsworth bequest.

LEFT OF FIREPLACE:

Henry Hoare of Mitcham Grove, father of Lydia, who married Thomas, 10th Bt, in 1808. Painted by Thomas Black (d. 1777).

Underneath this portrait hangs an oval chalk and watercolour portrait of *Agnes Acland*, daughter of the 11th Baronet.

RIGHT OF FIREPLACE:

A group of watercolours by Sir Thomas Dyke Acland, 11th Bt, and Miss St John Mildmay. The subjects are Killerton and Holnicote, the Aclands' Exmoor property, except for the painting in the top centre, which possibly depicts a French scene.

RIGHT OF ORGAN:

A group of chalk portraits of various members of the Acland family by Henry Singleton (1766–1839).

Mary Erskine, 2nd wife of Sir Thomas Dyke Acland, 11th Bt, by William Miller (1796–1882).

Eleanor Cropper, the wife of Sir Francis Acland, 14th Bt. A pastel drawing by Florence Small (1860–1933).

FURNITURE

The mahogany break-front glazed bookcase facing the fireplace was made for the house in 1808 by Mr Carter, an Exeter cabinetmaker. Most of the Acland furniture was put into store in Exeter for the duration of the Second World War, and this was one of the few pieces which survived the Exeter blitz in 1942.

In front of the fireplace is an early nineteenth-century mahogany-framed settee. The mahogany square piano by the door to the Corridor was made in 1817 by Muzio Clementi (1752–1832), who was also a leading pianist, composer and publisher of works by Beethoven.

You are welcome to play the grand piano, which was made by Bechstein in 1906–7.

CERAMICS

The break-front bookcase contains a collection of ceramics, some of which were acquired by the Acland family. The collection is made up chiefly of English eighteenth-century pieces, including part of a Chelsea dessert service marked with the red anchor *c*.1752–6. There are also oriental, French and Viennese pieces.

SCULPTURE

OVER DOOR TO LEFT OF ORGAN:

Marble bas-relief portrait of Sir Thomas Acland, 11th Bt, probably by Sir George Frampton (1860–1928).

Leave the Music Room by the door to the left of the organ, and turn left for the Drawing Room.

THE CORRIDOR

This originally led to the main front door of the house and has been very little altered since 1778. Its simplicity, good proportions and fine mahogany doors with elegant fanlights are typical of the work of John Johnson, the architect of Killerton.

At the opposite end of the corridor, and behind the glazed doors (the indoor entrance to the restaurant) were the servants' quarters. In the time of the Great Sir Thomas, the housekeeper was Mrs Craggs: 'She reigned supreme in the still room with the butler, ladies' maids etc. She had the first part of dinner in the servants' hall, but when it came to pudding, she headed the procession to walk out, each of them carrying their plate of pudding, across the passage, through the still room to the house-keeper's room.'

PICTURES

The original Grillion's Club portraits, from which the engravings in the Study were taken, hang here. They include W. E. Gladstone, Lord John Russell, drafter of the 1832 Reform Bill, and Lord Ashley (later Lord Shaftesbury), the originator of the Factory Acts and the Ragged Schools.

METALWORK

The lighted niche displays presentation plate, which probably graced the dining-table of Grillion's Hotel, where the meetings took place: the silver candlestick was presented to Sir Thomas in 1846, and the silver-gilt salver to his lifelong friend Robert Inglis, a Tory politician. On a minia-ture cushion is a mourning ring commemorating the death in 1785 of Sir Thomas, 7th Bt, who rebuilt Killerton.

CLOCK

The large mantel clock was made by Richard Gibson of London. It has a six tune selector, which plays every three hours on the hour.

THE DRAWING ROOM

This impressive room belongs to the period of Sir Charles Acland, 12th Bt, who made sweeping changes to Killerton in 1900. He moved the main entrance away from this side of the house, pulled down the old front lobby (formerly an extension of the Corridor), and opened it up into the adjoining breakfast parlour (Drawing Room). The columns and beams show where load-bearing walls were removed, and the door into the garden indicates the position of the old front entrance. Henry Protheroe of Cheltenham, the architect, took pains to keep the new work in harmony with the old. The replacement fireplaces came from a firm in Bond Street, and Jackson & Son were employed to decorate the original plain ceilings.

In the end, this grand room was properly used only for the short period before the First World War. In the 1920s and '30s it stood empty, except for rows of gilt ballroom chairs in brown holland dustcovers, and it came to life only on rare occasions. An entry in the 14th Baronet's year-book for 1927 states: 'Our dance. About 235 people. Just enough supper and room to dance and sit out ... Cubby [son of the 14th Baronet] made about 8 bowls of spring flowers.' The room was redecorated by the National Trust in 1996.

PICTURES

CLOCKWISE, FROM THE DOOR LEFT OF THE CORRIDOR:

A large watercolour of an Italian landscape by Francis Nicholson (1753–1844).

Lady Harriet Acland, neé Fox-Strangways (d. 1815) by Sir Joshua Reynolds (1723–92). She was the wife of Colonel John Dyke Acland, the 9th Baronet's brother who in 1777 succeeded in securing her husband's release from the Americans during the War of Independence. On the stand beneath the portrait this dramatic event is portrayed.

Lady Harriet Acland crossing the Hudson by Robert Pollard (1755–1838).

Sir Thomas Dyke Acland, 7th Bt (1722–85) by Sir Joshua Reynolds (1723–92). He was the builder of Killerton. He is shown in the blue coat of the North Devon Staghounds, of which he was Master for nearly 30 years, and with one of his hounds. The portrait was bought by the National Trust with the help of a Heritage Lottery grant.

Colonel John Dyke Acland (1746–78). He was the eldest son of the 7th Baronet who in 1770 married Lady Harriet Fox-Strangways. He took an active role in the American War of Independence during which he was captured by the enemy. Due to her intercession he was released by the Americans and resumed his parliamentary career only to die from a chill caught after fighting a duel at the age of 32.

Hannah More (1745–1833) by Henry Pickersgill (1782–1875). She was an evangelical Christian edu-cationalist, playwright, poet and a zealous worker for the abolition of the Slave Trade: the letter by her side is addressed to William Wilberforce, the

The Corridor

The Drawing Room

triumphant champion of the cause. Her religious writings were much admired by the Great Sir Thomas, 'that most despotic of tyrants, and most ardent of friends', who commissioned this portrait 'against my most earnest remonstrances and positive refusals'. Sir Thomas's mother was unimpressed: 'I think her the most scrutinising artful countenance I have seen, rather vulgar in manner, at least certainly not polished.'

Sir Thomas Acland, 10th Bt (1787–1871), *Lydia, Lady Acland and their son Thomas*, by Henry Singleton (1766–1839). The three are shown full-length at a piano which is the same Broadwood Grand that stands in front of the picture.

Maria Acland, and her son Hugh, by Samuel Woodford (1763–1817). She was the wife of Sir Henry Hugh Hoare, 3rd Bt. Their son, here shown aged seven, later became the 4th Baronet.

The Pastor's Fireside by Henry Singleton (1766–1839). The painting shows the children of Sir Thomas, 10th Bt, being read to by the vicar of Silverton. Amongst his ten children, Thomas the eldest became the 11th Baronet, Baldwin entered the Navy and died at sea, Leopold joined the church and Henry became Regius Professor of Medicine at Oxford. Harriet and Reginald died young. John Barton, who is depicted next to the dog, emigrated to New Zealand with the Rector's son Charles Tripp where they farmed 110,000 acres. The older man seated behind the vicar is reputedly the artist.

Charlotte Mordaunt by John Downman (1750–1824). The watercolour depicts Charlotte, the cousin of Mary Mordaunt, first wife of the 11th Baronet.

Gertrude, Lady Acland by W.H. Funk, painted *c.*1890. She was the wife of Sir Charles Acland, 12th Bt. In the background to the portrait are the hills of Holnicote, the Aclands' Exmoor estate. She was a keen gardener who directed the restoration of the garden at Killerton at the end of the nineteenth century.

Sir Richard Colt Hoare (1758–1838), English School, *c.*1810. He lived at Stourhead and was a half-brother of Lydia, wife of the 10th Baronet. Frequent visits were made between Killerton and Stourhead, where both owners were developing their gardens and exchanging plants and ideas.

Sir Richard Hoare (1709–54). This portrait was probably completed by one of his daughters. Sir Richard was the father of Henrietta, wife of the 9th Baronet.

Sir Charles Acland, 12th Bt (1842–1919) by Sir Hubert von Herkomer (1849–1914). Writing to her brother-in-law in 1923, Eleanor Acland described Sir Charles's impact on Killerton: 'Uncle Charlie was very much undervitalised; awfully good and dutiful, and conscientiously trying to live up to the older standards … for a few years he and Aunt Gertie bustled and fussed about, bought new furniture, altered the house from top to toe.'

General Sir Hildebrand Oakes, 1st Bt (1754–1822). Attributed to George Romney (1734–1802). Oakes was born in Exeter and appointed Civil Commissioner for Malta in 1810. Family tradition claims he served with John Acland in America. He was created a Baronet in 1813.

Lydia Malortie, Mrs Henry Hoare (1754–1816) by George Romney (1734–1802). She married Henry in 1775. Their eldest child was Lydia, who married the 10th Baronet.

Henry Hoare of Mitcham Grove (1750–1828) by George Romney (1734–1802). He was father-in-law to the Great Sir Thomas and senior partner in the family bank.

FURNITURE

The Broadwood grand piano is reputed to be the earliest surviving six octave Broadwood piano in the country. It was made in 1802 and its serial number is 2355. The piano had been lost for over 30 years and was discovered in 1994 in the loft of one of the buildings on the estate. How it got there and why is something we may never know, but it is now happily back where it belongs.

Lady Harriet Acland crossing the Hudson to plead for her wounded husband's release during the American War of Independence; painted by Robert Pollard (Drawing Room)

CERAMICS

The large dish on the table is Dutch delft dating from *c*.1650. It depicts scenes from the life of Christ.

THE LIBRARY

The Library, and the Dining Room which opens out beyond it, were the 'Parlours', or principal rooms in the house, when Johnson designed them in 1778. They look much as they did then, although their use has altered more than once. The Library was at first the 'Little Parlour' and considered too brightly lit by Henrietta Acland, the 9th Baronet's wife. In 1806 she wrote to her son with news of the solution she proposed:

I am going to chuse a paper for Killerton – it occurred to me this morning – whether to shut up the three windows – or shut up the two and have a colonnade before the three to keep [out] the Western Sun which is very insufferable in the Summer … I think a paper in pannels with Antique ornaments and Etruscan figures will have a good effect as there are no pictures.

This wallpaper has long since disappeared and the room was most recently redecorated by the National Trust in 2002.

Later, this room was used as a drawing room, until Sir Charles decided to turn it into a library as part of his Edwardian alterations. Shelving was then moved from elsewhere in the house, the ceiling was decorated like those in the Drawing Room and the Music Room, and Mr Protheroe produced another period fireplace. Latterly, this lovely room, with its glorious views of the garden, was a haven of peace where it was possible to read or write letters, away from the bustle in the rest of the house.

BOOKS

In 1923 the 14th Baronet's wife wrote, '[The Library] reflects a serious somewhat heavy library taste; economy and caution too, for there are few first editions, and they don't generally seem to have bought a book till it was well established as a proper book to have.' Today, the Library houses part of the collection of the Rev. Sabine Baring-Gould (1834–1924), parson and squire of Lewtrenchard near Okehampton, and author of the hymn 'Onward, Christian Soldiers'.

To the right of the Dining Room door there is an amusing set of false book-spines, with names such as *Nettles with Nice Noses* and *Paper Currency Exploded*.

PICTURES

RIGHT OF THE FIREPLACE:

Sir Francis Acland, 14th Bt (1874–1939), copied from a photograph, by John Berrie (1887–1962).

Supposed portrait of *Sir John Acland, 1st Bt* (*c*.1591–1647). Despite the label, this portrait was painted about 1700, and so cannot be of the 1st Baronet. It

The Library

may show another John Acland (d. 1703), the son of the 5th Baronet and father of the 6th Baronet.

Pencil sketch of *Ellen Acland* (1913–24), daughter of Sir Francis Acland, 14th Bt, and his wife Eleanor. Ellen was killed in a road accident outside the front gates of Killerton.

Hugh Radcliffe (d. 1553). English School. Radcliffe of Stepney and the Middle Temple was the father of Margaret who married John Acland MP in the early part of the sixteenth century. Margaret's dowry added to the accumulated wealth of the Aclands.

Sir Thomas Acland, 7th Bt. (1722–85). English School. He rebuilt Killerton in 1778–9.

Archduke John of Austria (1782–1859) by A.J.B. Lampi. The Archduke was the youngest brother of the Austrian Emperor and a moderately unsuccessful general during the Napoleonic Wars.

FURNITURE

Beneath the portrait of the 14th Baronet is an early nineteenth-century rosewood writing bureau, together with a privately published book about Ellen Acland's brief life.

In the centre of the room is a circular rosewood tip-top breakfast-table, 1820.

The set of mahogany armchairs with green leather seats is dated *c.*1800. They are on loan to Killerton.

SCULPTURE

OVER TWO OF THE DOORS:

Night and Morning, terracotta roundels by the great Danish Neo-classical sculptor Bertel Thorvaldsen

Morning: a terracotta roundel by Bertel Thorvaldsen in the Library

(1770–1844). He was living in Rome when the Great Sir Thomas and his wife visited the Mediterranean in their yacht in 1836. Lady Acland played and sang to Thorvaldsen, and these roundels were brought back as keepsakes.

CLOCK

On the mantelpiece is a French white marble bracket clock of classical form dating from the early nineteenth century.

THE DINING ROOM

Johnson designed this room as the 'Great Parlour', and he enriched it accordingly with a frieze (his sole piece of ornamental plasterwork) and the handsome pair of carved wooden columns, which frames the double doors into the Library. For a time, in the nineteenth century, this room was the Library, but Sir Charles, 12th Bt, turned it into the Dining Room in the Edwardian period. He adorned the ceiling with medallions of the four main agricultural operations – Ploughing, Sowing, Hoeing and Reaping – and portrait heads of himself and his wife. In this case, Mr Mears, a local plasterer and protégé of Lady Acland, was employed instead of a specialist firm.

In the Victorian era of the 10th Baronet, dinner was always late in the evening, often at 10 pm or later, and Sunday lunch was clearly a memorable occasion, as his granddaughter, Agnes, recalled:

After Sunday morning service, grandpapa walked through the kitchen gardens and at a certain point near the greenhouse received bunches of violets which he presented to ladies of the party. The party then went slowly on and finally up the drive to Killerton. Then we had a big meal, a sirloin of beef at one end, two chickens at the other … Then after this ample meal, and after coffee we proceeded to church. At times grandpapa slept during the sermon – tradition said he woke up once and said 'Hear! Hear!' thinking he was in the House of Commons.

Within recent memory, all meals except tea took place in this room. By the 1930s there was no longer a butler; nevertheless, there were two parlourmaids who spent two hours every morning polishing silver, and clean, starched table napkins appeared at every meal. In summer, the windows were often

The Dining Room

open and Sir Francis would step out at breakfast time to give corn to the tame pheasant which came strutting down the lawn. In winter the room was very cold. Evening dress with bare arms was the rule for ladies, and it was a much-coveted privilege to sit on the side of the table nearest to the fire.

PICTURES

The paintings were rehung in 2003 following redecoration.

CLOCKWISE FROM OVER THE DOOR TO
THE CORRIDOR:

Sir Arthur Acland (d.1610), probably English School. Arthur died as a young man, leaving a son, Sir John, 1st Bt.

Sir Hugh Acland, 6th Bt (1697–1728), attributed to Jonathan Richardson (1664–1745). Sir Hugh married the heiress Cecily Wroth in 1721, which united the considerable fortunes of the Acland, Wroth and Palmer families.

Elizabeth Acland (1700–38), English School. She was the sister of Sir Hugh, 6th Bt, who married Sir John Davie.

Sir John Acland, 1st Bt (*c*.1591–1647) by Robert Walker (1607–58). During the Civil War he was a staunch Royalist, who garrisoned his home, Columbjohn, in Charles's favour. He was knighted for his services and appointed sheriff of the county.

Colonel Palmer (d. 1684), English School. Related to the 6th Baronet's wife, Cecily Wroth.

Elizabeth, Lady Wroth (*c*.1650–70) by Sir Peter Lely (1618–80).

Sir Hugh Acland, 5th Bt (1637–1713) by Sir Peter Lely (1618–1680) and his studio. The fourth son of the 1st Baronet, he inherited the title at the age of 18. He married Anne Daniel, the heiress daughter of a Yorkshire knight. In 1688 he became a Tory MP.

Elizabeth, Lady Acland, attributed to a follower of Sir Anthony Van Dyck, 1644. She was the wife of the 1st Baronet and daughter of Sir Francis Vincent.

John Acland (d. 1703) by Sir William Gandy (*c.*1655–1729). The son of the 5th Baronet, but predeceased his father.

Anne, Lady Acland, English School. The daughter of Sir Thomas Daniel and wife of the 5th Baronet.

*Sir John Morley, c.*1631 and his wife *Cicely Caryll, Lady Morley*, both English School.

Sir Hugh Acland (1637–1713), attributed to William Gandy (*c.*1655–1729).

Sir John Acland, 1st Bt (*c.*1591–1647), English School. But possibly John Acland (d. 1703), son of the 5th Baronet.

Sir William Morley, Bt (d.1701), attributed to Samuel van Hoogstraeten(1627–78), *c.*1662.

Anne Denham, Lady Morley, by Sir Peter Lely (1618– 1680), *c.*1631. First wife of Sir William.

Mary, Lady Morley by Cornelius Johnson (1593–1661), 1631. The daughter of Sir Robert Heath and an ancestor of Cecily Wroth who married Sir Hugh Acland, 6th Bt.

Margaret, Lady Heath by Cornelius Johnson (1593–1661), *c.*1630. She married Sir Robert Heath and was an ancestor of Cecily, Lady Acland, the wife of Sir Hugh Acland, 6th Bt. Sir Robert Heath was an MP and Attorney-General who presided over the Star Chamber presentations in 1629–30.

Sir Francis Vincent, 1st Bt, English School, 1618. The father of Elizabeth, wife of Sir John Acland, 1st Bt.

Sir Francis Acland, 2nd Bt (d. 1649), English School.

*Sir Richard Acland, c.*1720, in the manner of Michael Dahl (1646–1723). The brother of the 6th Baronet. His daughter became the second wife of Sir Richard Hoare, 1st Bt of Barn Elms, Surrey.

Mary Morley, Countess of Derby, in the manner of Michael Dahl (1646–1723).

*Mary Osbaldiston, Lady Wroth, c.*1700, by Michael Dahl (1646–1723). The mother of Cecily Wroth, wife of Sir Hugh Acland, 6th Bt.

Sir Hugh Acland, 6th Bt (1697–1728), English School.

Cecilia Morley by Michael Dahl (1646–1723). The daughter of Sir John Morley, she married Francis Osbaldiston.

FURNITURE

Mahogany sideboard, four drawers with lion mask drop handles, turned legs and claw feet. Irish, late eighteenth-century.

Pair of George III side-tables with satinwood veneered tops.

Mahogany dining-table with turned legs and brass castors, 1820.

Set of mahogany dining-chairs, early nineteenth-century.

Pair of rosewood folio cabinets with Italian marble tops, made for this room in the early nineteenth century.

CERAMICS

On the sideboard and the two lower shelves of the dumb waiter is part of the Chelsea dessert service, also on display in the Music Room. On the top shelf of the dumb waiter is a Bow circular basket, 1760. The two chargers on the folio cabinets are Chinese.

The porcelain on the dining-table is Minton, 1820.

SILVER

ON DINING-TABLE:

Set of four George III sauce tureens and covers, with lion mask handles, the sides engraved with the quartered Acland/Hoare coats of arms to commemorate the marriage of the Great Sir Thomas.

Leave the Dining Room by the door to the left of the fireplace, cross the Corridor, and turn left up the stairs.

THE STAIRCASE

An archway leads to the massive oak staircase, which was part of Charles and Gertrude Acland's plan to make Killerton into a grand Edwardian house. Here, ladies in sweeping evening gowns could descend in full view of the gentlemen warming themselves in front of the fire. The design of the staircase is hardly in sympathy with the rest of the house, but the breadth and solidity of construction serve its purpose well.

The Staircase Hall

PICTURES

AT FOOT OF STAIRS:

Thomas Dyke Acland, 11th Bt (1809–98), a chalk drawing by George Richmond, dated 1854. The drawing to its right, also by Richmond, is of an unknown sitter.

ON THE STAIRS:

Francis Nicholson (1753–1844). A self portrait aged 89. Nicholson was a founder member of the Society of Painters in Watercolours, who taught painting to Henrietta, mother of the 10th Baronet.

Matthew Fortescue (1754–1842), English School. He married Henrietta, Lady Acland, in 1795 following the death of the 9th Baronet. As the Great Sir Thomas's stepfather, he greatly influenced his childhood.

Henrietta Hoare, Lady Acland, later Mrs Fortescue (d. 1841), English School. She was the mother of the Great Sir Thomas, who shared her second husband's stern outlook. In 1806, on Thomas's

departure from Oxford, she wrote 'Let your joy be rational and contained within due bounds, let it be the feeling of a man of sense, not of a wild inconsiderate schoolboy, whatever you do, be on your guard – make no promises you may repent of hereafter and see with your eyes open, not through a glass darkly'. Six years later, his progress was disappointing, and she issued a reprimand:

> 'I have heard of you making morning visits when people are at dinner, that is all very good fun for a School Boy, but not proper for Sir Thomas Acland who I hope to see member for the County … will you remember you are within a few days of being five and twenty – surely that is an age one may expect steadiness if it is ever to arrive at all.'

Henrietta was a talented artist, and several of her watercolours are on display in the house.

Sir Thomas Dyke Acland, 9th Bt (1752–94), English School.

The Great Sir Thomas, 10th Bt (1787–1871), by William Owen (1769–1825). This huge full-length portrait was painted in 1818 after Sir Thomas's only election defeat in a long Parliamentary career. It shows him standing near the hustings in the castle grounds at Exeter with a speech in his hand. The picture was known to later generations as 'Grandpapa in a Thunderstorm'.

Lydia Hoare, Lady Acland (1786–1856), English School. She married the 10th Baronet in 1808. He outlived her by fifteen years.

Holnicote from the South-West, 1785, by Francis Towne (1739–1816). Holnicote was the Exmoor estate given to the National Trust by Sir Richard Acland in 1944. In the foreground is Sir Thomas Dyke Acland, 9th Bt, returning from a hunt with his stag hounds.

Captain Charles Acland (1812–37), English School. He was a Captain in the Royal Navy who died at sea of blackwater fever off the coast of Africa.

Killerton Park, attributed to William Tomkins (c.1732–92). In the middle ground is a white painted Gothic folly which has long since disappeared.

LIGHTING

The alabaster light-fitting dates from the 1920s and was designed by the architect Randall Wells for another house.

THE COSTUME COLLECTION

The top landing leads to the exceptional Costume Collection which is one of Killerton's special attractions. During the Second World War, Paulise de Bush was able to save many eighteenth- and nineteenth-century costumes from an old house in Berkshire, when they were about to be thrown away, and this was the beginning of her collection which she left to the National Trust on her death. Around 9,000 items of costume are now housed at Killerton, and more than fifty different costumes are exhibited every year, in rooms named after one-time Acland estates – Efford, near Bude, Landkey and Bray in North Devon, and Trerice near Newquay. The displays are changed annually.

Retrace your steps to the front door, and on leaving the house, turn left, following the wall round to the entrance of the Laundry.

The Laundry

An eighteenth-century quilted petticoat, brocade shoes and an Italian fan, from the Killerton costume collection

THE LAUNDRY

Until it closed in 1940, Killerton Laundry provided employment for three full-time female staff, and a varying number of part-time staff. The first room entered is the drying room, where the laundry process ended. On wet days, clothes and linen could be dried here on the racks which pull out from the wall. On the table under the window, irons of every shape and size were used to smooth and finish items ready to be returned to the house. In the 1930s, a woman was paid four pence an hour to iron the starched damask napkins for the dining-table. Next door, in the wash-house, dirty items could be boiled up with grated soap in the two coppers, and then scrubbed and starched to achieve the effect required by contemporary fashions. (For a fuller description, see the separate Laundry leaflet.)

On leaving the Laundry, turn right and retrace your steps towards the front door of the house. On the far side of the forecourt is the entrance to the garden.

THE GARDEN

The garden was created by two remarkable dynasties: the Aclands, owners of Killerton since the early seventeenth century; and the Veitch family, nurserymen and landscapers from the mid-eighteenth century until recent times, whose plant introductions have changed the English countryside.

By 1801 a pleasure ground had been fenced off from the landscape park, begun in 1772, when John Veitch was taken on by Sir Thomas Dyke Acland, 7th Bt. Veitch soon recognised that this garden had a remarkable microclimate: with sloping lawns inclined to the sun, it contained no frost pockets and was sheltered from any cold north winds by Dolbury Hill, known locally as 'Killerton Clump'. The lime-free soil (pH 4.5–5.5) made the garden particularly suitable for plants such as camellias, magnolias and rhododendrons.

The garden was subsequently developed in the 'Gardenesque' style – a term coined by the eminent horticultural writer J. C. Loudon in 1832. Even before that date, this style existed in the garden at Killerton, with its winding paths, scattered flower-beds, shrubberies, specimen trees and shrubs. Many of these were exotics introduced by the Veitch nursery and planted to show off colourful flowers

and the rarest varieties to their best advantage. The garden was further ornamented by features in the various styles of the day: the Picturesque predominated with buildings of rustic woodwork such as the Bear's Hut (4), but there were also assorted elements of Greek Revival or Italianate, such as the splendid orangery (removed in 1937), various fine vases and a formal flower garden where the Forecourt (1) is now.

Enriched by the exotics introduced by the Veitch family (many of them first grown in this country at Killerton), the garden today still has very much the character of a Regency pleasure ground.

THE VEITCH CONNECTION

John Veitch was born in 1752 in Ancrum near Jedburgh, the son of Thomas Veitch, a nurseryman. We do not know how or where he learnt to lay out grounds, but between leaving home in 1766 and arriving at Killerton he had become sufficiently skilled to be recommended to the 7th Baronet. Sir Thomas appointed him agent for all his West Country estates and allowed him also to set up his own nursery at Budlake on the Killerton Estate and to act as a freelance landscaper. Such a generous arrangement was doubtless the mark of a liberal employer, but it was also pragmatic: Veitch must have known that his skills could command at least a modest fortune on the open market, and Sir Thomas have realised that he had little hope of retaining the services of his talented employee unless he allowed him some freedom.

Veitch's career at Killerton spanned many years, during which taste in landscape design saw a number of revolutionary changes. He remained active well into his eighties, dying in 1839, two years after the accession of Queen Victoria. During that time, the smooth and simple style of 'Capability' Brown had given way to the garden style of Humphry Repton, which allowed more complexity, with shrubberies, flower-beds and formal areas near the house. These often included specialised gardens

(Left) Killerton in 1818. The garden still has the character of a Regency pleasure ground; from a coloured engraving by D. Havell after L. E. Reed

John Veitch, who became head gardener at Killerton in 1772 and went on to found the famous dynasty of nurserymen and landscape gardeners

of, for example, roses or American plants. The rugged Picturesque landscape style championed by the Aclands' friend William Sawrey Gilpin and the Gardenesque style of Loudon, designed to show the beauty of the individual plants, were already starting to be replaced by the grand formal gardens typical of the Victorian age.

According to Veitch's grandson, Thomas Beatty, he 'laid out grounds in every County in England except the little County of Rutland'. If true, Veitch would be among the most prolific and important landscapers of the late eighteenth and early nineteenth centuries. However, little is recorded about the parks and gardens he made. We know that for some Veitch was the sole designer and creator, but in others, perhaps the majority, he implemented the recommendations of other designers such as Repton, organising a work-force and ordering supplies of tens of thousands of trees and shrubs from nurseries throughout Great Britain.

The coming-of-age of Sir Thomas Acland, 10th Bt, in 1808 marked the beginning of the most important phase of the garden's evolution. Its rapid development under Veitch's direction, including the planting of Sweet Chestnuts and the creation of the Bear's Hut (4), Beech Walk and Ice-House (9), all within a few months, suggests the impatience of the young baronet and his bride Lydia, a cousin of the Hoares of Stourhead, for a mature garden.

In 1813 John Veitch gave the nursery plus £5,000 to his eldest son James. It was probably James and the other younger Veitches who made the nursery predominant in the importation of exotic garden plants, while John continued his work on the Acland estates and acted as salesman for the nursery's plants at many great estates throughout the country where gardens were in the making. The nursery flourished throughout Victorian times, becoming the largest and most prestigious in the land. It sent plant-hunters such as the brothers William and Thomas Lobb, Charles Maries and Ernest 'Chinese' Wilson around the world, often to areas never previously visited by Europeans. Many of the plants they sent back were grown at Killerton soon after they were introduced, such as *Thuja plicata*, *Cryptomeria japonica* 'Lobbii' and *Chamaecyparis obtusa*.

THE TWENTIETH CENTURY

The garden changed little during the late nineteenth century, but the accession of the 12th Baronet, Sir Charles Dyke Acland, in 1898 brought another era of garden improvement, instigated largely by his wife Gertrude. A keen gardener of twenty years at Holnicote before moving to Killerton, she was an ardent follower of another Gertrude, Gertrude Jekyll, and was committed to making both the house and garden grander, calling in William Robinson, author of *The English Flower Garden* (1883), to advise. The double row of rhododendrons separating garden from park was replaced by the formal terrace and herbaceous border, and the Rock Garden (6) was created in what had been an old quarry behind the Bear's Hut. The head

Killerton Garden

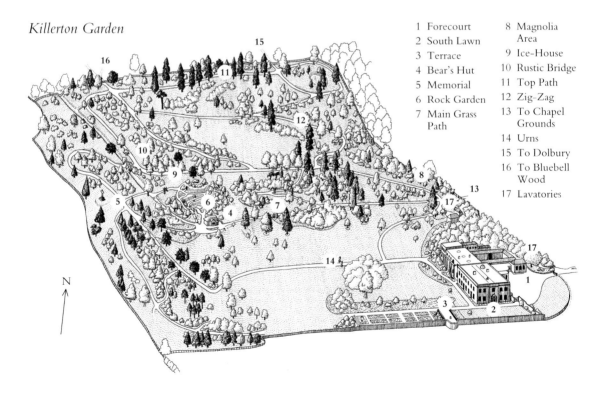

1 Forecourt
2 South Lawn
3 Terrace
4 Bear's Hut
5 Memorial
6 Rock Garden
7 Main Grass Path
8 Magnolia Area
9 Ice-House
10 Rustic Bridge
11 Top Path
12 Zig-Zag
13 To Chapel Grounds
14 Urns
15 To Dolbury
16 To Bluebell Wood
17 Lavatories

The Terrace

gardener responsible for implementing these improvements was John Coutts, later to become Curator at Kew.

During the 1920s and '30s Sir Francis Dyke Acland continued to improve the garden, replanting and adding species of rhododendron from Kingdon-Ward's expeditions to the Himalayas. It was Sir Francis who first opened the garden to the public, a tradition which the National Trust has continued.

TOUR OF THE GARDEN

1 THE FORECOURT

This was the site of a small formal flower garden shown in the Exeter artist John Gendall's *Fragments of Killerton* (1831). The house and walls are now dominated by wisterias and Banksian roses with a border of autumn- and winter-flowering plants at the base; liriopes are followed by winter-flowering shrubs, finishing with Lenten hellebores.

Until about 1900 there was no ha-ha here, and the parkland ran right up to the house. Iron railings close to the house often failed to prevent cattle from eating the wall-plants. The gravel area, made necessary by the increasing use of cars, was raked every morning until as late as 1935.

The armillary sphere was installed to commemorate Sir Richard Acland, 15th Bt (1906–90), who donated the Killerton estate to the National Trust.

2 THE SOUTH LAWN

Around the corner of the house, the Bear's Hut (4) can just be seen at the top of the lawn and also a fine Weeping Silver Lime. The large clump of rhododendrons below the central path was probably a part of John Veitch's 1808–9 planting and includes old hardy hybrid rhododendrons such as *R. smithii*, commonly know as 'Cornish Red' and the largest hardy variety, capable of reaching 10m (33ft). On the western edge of the lawn there is a very fine *Quercus* × *hispanica* 'Lucombeana' (the Lucombe Oak raised by William Lucombe of St Thomas's,

25

Exeter, in about 1765). The ha-ha at the foot of the lawn, made in the 1970s by the National Trust, leads the eye on into the park without interruption.

3 THE TERRACE

Suggested in 1900 by the architect Henry Protheroe, this was completed to the recommendations of William Robinson in 1905. The head gardener, John Coutts, mocked the plans for the Terrace wall, saying that it began nowhere and ended nowhere; the building of a ha-ha from either end of the Terrace incorporated it more satisfactorily into the garden.

Near the house a lawn and a border of tender perennials run along the outer edge, while the further half of the Terrace has beds of roses and perennials on an axis between two magnificent Coade stone vases dated 1805. Separating this from the rest of the garden is a generous herbaceous border, a hallmark of Robinson's style, with flowers ranging from blue and yellow nearest the house, through hot colours, to pink and white with grey foliage at the furthest end.

In 1926 Lloyd George addressed a rally of 19,000 people from the central alcove of the Terrace at the launch of his new Land Policy. Today it is the site of a replica of an eighteenth-century sundial engraved by Benjamin Martin of London.

4 THE BEAR'S HUT

This was built by John Veitch as a surprise for Lydia Acland, wife of the 10th Baronet, on the Aclands' return from their honeymoon in 1808. It was often called the Hermit's Hut until used to house a pet

The Bear's Hut from the Rock Garden

black bear brought back from Canada in the 1860s by Gilbert, brother of Sir Charles Dyke Acland, later 12th Bt. The floor is partly paved with small deer knuckle-bones. Jane Loudon in her book *Gardening for Ladies* (1846) commented that this appeared to her 'decidedly in bad taste'. She also mentioned that such huts generally had windows of stained glass; that in the Bear's Hut windows was collected by the Acland family on their travels.

5 THE MEMORIAL

Erected to commemorate Sir Thomas Dyke Acland, 10th Bt, in 1873 by 40 of his friends, whose names surround the base of the cross, this commands fine views to the west towards Dartmoor. The gentle dome of Cosdon Beacon, one of the most northerly parts of Dartmoor, can be seen on a clear day 20 miles away to the west. The large white building about two miles away to the south-west is Rewe rectory, designed by James Knowles in 1844, and the farm about a mile off in the same direction is Columb John Farm.

The landscape in the foreground, known as West Park, was originally planned by W. S. Gilpin in the early nineteenth century as a patchwork of fields surrounded by hedges and dotted with clumps of trees. More intensive farming in the twentieth century rooted out these features to create huge prairie-like fields, but now a return to the former traditional landscape is under way, with tree-planting and a return to permanent pasture.

The prevailing south-westerly winds are a continuing threat to the mature trees in the garden. Despite the shelter belt, 80 trees were lost in the gale of 25 January 1990. As you look away from the garden, the shelter belt running up to the garden fence to the left of the view has been deepened and thickened recently by incorporating a much larger wind break. North and east of this viewpoint, many trees were lost, and the shelter belt has been re-established behind the path.

6 THE ROCK GARDEN

Previously a quarry, this was developed as a rock garden in 1905 by John Coutts. A sun trap in summer, water was introduced in 1989. The Sweet Chestnuts around the top date from Veitch's original planting of 1808. Intensively planted in its early years, the Rock Garden was the passion of Gertrude, wife of the 12th Baronet. Four gardeners tended it full-time, extra women being employed in the autumn to remove fallen leaves from the plants. The Goyle (a Devon word for a dark sunken path) runs around the west side of the Rock Garden against the early deer-park wall.

7 THE MAIN GRASS PATH

The area surrounding the Grass Path from the Bear's Hut to the house contains some of the cream of Killerton's plant collection. On the upper side of the path are young Cork Oaks, with another older specimen to the east. Towards the house are three trees which are the largest of their species in the British Isles: *Stewartia pseudocamellia* has stunning bark and is interesting in every month of the year; looking uphill and slightly to the right, just beyond a clump of camellias, one can see the conifer *Taiwania cryptomerioïdes*; just to its right and further away, is the deciduous *Liquidambar formosana*. Closer still to the house you get an excellent view of the lower part of the garden; nearby is a very dense upright form of *Libocedrus decurrens*. Killerton's spring bulbs are seen at their best along the length of the Grass Path.

8 THE MAGNOLIA AREA

Uphill from the east end of the grass path is an area notable for its magnolias. Of particular interest are a *Magnolia campbellii* so large that when in flower it can be seen over three miles away, from the road to Exeter, and *Magnolia wilsonii* with its scented flowers in early summer.

9 THE ICE-HOUSE

Built in 1808, this is large enough to hold 40 tons of ice, enough for two or three years' supply. When first used in 1809, it took 30 men five days to fill. At this period, cold winters were more frequent and ice could be taken from the River Culm or from a pond in the park. Once inside, the ice would be crushed to pack it more tightly and would congeal

Embothrium coccineum *and* Rhododendron arboreum

hemlocks. The glimpse down between tall rhododendrons across the Beech Walk to the lower garden is known as Lady Gertrude's Glade after the 12th Baronet's wife. The loss of some large trees in the 1990 gale has opened up fine views: Woodbury Common can be seen to the south-east. The fine southerly view takes in the mouth of the Exe estuary almost fifteen miles away. A gate and a stile lead out of the garden from the top path: from the lower one, the path turns left to the Bluebell Wood, which leads directly to Columb John; the upper one leads to the top of Dolbury Hill, with its remains of Iron Age fortifications.

12 THE ZIG-ZAG

Descending towards the house, the zig-zag path passes two fine Sweet Chestnuts from Veitch's original planting and then a Californian Coast Redwood, which is the tallest tree in the garden; it was raised from the first sending of seed about 1843 and planted in 1860. Below this is the tree with the largest girth in the garden, a Wellingtonia, planted in 1858. Named after the Duke of Wellington 'because it stood above its fellows', it was also raised from the first introduction of seed of this species, in 1853.

The path divides at the small thatched building (now lavatories), which was once a dairy. The downhill path to the south-west returns to the house and restaurant; the latter contains a photograph of the orangery which once stood nearby. Built between 1808 and 1826, this was similar in design to examples by Repton's sons George Stanley and John Adey Repton. Its symmetrical design gave a degree of formality to this part of the garden, and its Greek Revival detailing was echoed by other classical ornamentation on the west front of the house and the urns which flank the main path. The path to the east leaves the garden via a turnstile, from where the Chapel may be approached via a level walk. Alternatively, visitors may return to the stable block.

into a solid mass. Ice could then be broken off using a pickaxe and transported to the kitchen in zinc-lined boxes, to be used for chilling drinks or to produce iced desserts.

10 THE RUSTIC BRIDGE

The bridge, first constructed in 1808, was rebuilt in the 1980s to bear the weight of garden vehicles. The ha-ha, dating back at least to the mid-eighteenth century, formerly had a paling fence along its crest designed to keep deer in the park. It runs for over three-quarters of a mile, ending at the River Culm.

11 THE TOP PATH

Lined with deciduous azaleas, attractive both in spring bloom and autumn colour, this passes through a grove of Californian Redwoods and

THE PARK, WOODLAND AND ESTATE

The backbone of the park is Killerton Clump, an outcrop of volcanic rock which gives the hill its distinctive shape; the older name, Dolbury, has a Saxon origin, and there are traces of Iron Age civilisation (400BC) in the earthworks on top of the hill. (In recent times, part of the Clump has been designated a Site of Special Scientific Interest.) The park was first laid out in the 1770s, when Sir Thomas Acland, 7th Bt, decided to rebuild Killerton House. With John Veitch as his landscape adviser, he took over the farmland immediately surrounding the Clump and diverted the main Exeter road so as to make an imposing setting for his fine new house. The oldest trees in the park date from this time, as does the pond, which made a convenient drinking-place for the fallow deer.

THE STABLES

The stable block by John Johnson – one of the most distinguished buildings on the estate – was completed a year later than the house, and in 1780 the bell in the turret-clock, cast by Thomas Bilbie of Cullompton, began to sound the hour as it still does to this day.

COLUMB JOHN

Of the many paths by which visitors can explore the Clump, one of the most interesting leads through the woods to Columb John, This is the site of a former Acland mansion, which was garrisoned for the King in the Civil War, and is marked by the ruined archway of the gatehouse and a small

The Stables

(restored) chapel of St John. (Columb John Farm, the oldest farm on the estate, is private. Visitors are asked to keep to the marked paths.) Columb John chapel is now seldom used.

THE CHAPEL

A path to the east from the former dairy leads from the garden to Killerton chapel, which the Great Sir Thomas built in 1841 in 'Lady Acland's Shrubbery' (newly named the 'Chapel Ground') to replace Columb John chapel. The architect C. R. Cockerell (1788–1863) produced an ambitious design in accordance with his client's wishes. To Cockerell's annoyance, it was to be based on the Norman Chapel of St Joseph of Arimathea at Glastonbury, as he stated in a letter to Sir Thomas in 1838: 'If this finds you at Killerton & still bent on Joseph of Glastonbury, do not think of neutralizing, castrating & emasculating the copy of that noble building, & flattering yourself that you have what will be worthy of the original – either have an original work altogether or a correct reproduction.'

The Chapel

Inside, Sir Thomas commissioned a special seat for himself, on the right-hand side towards the east end, and other members of the family were involved too – one son, Arthur, designed and carved the neo-Norman stone altar, while another son, Henry, applied his Ruskinian taste to the design of the capitals. The west rose window was based on Barfeston in Kent. *A fuller description is provided by the leaflet available in the Chapel.*

Several of the fine trees here predate the Chapel, including two splendid Tulip trees from a grove planted in 1808. These are 'champion' trees – the largest in this country. Also of particular interest are two magnificent hybrid oaks planted at the same time – the rare *Quercus × hispanica* 'Suberosa' and *Q. × hispanica* 'Lucombeana' – and a fine specimen of *Ostrya carpinifolia* (Hop Hornbeam).

THE LODGE

Cockerell also designed the lodge at the entrance to the park. Here lived, rent-free, a pensioner whose duties were to open the drive gate at the sound of the coachman's whistle and to feed the ducks on the pond. These were supposed to nest in the stone 'Duck House' on the island, built in the 1850s when the place became a burial ground for family dogs. Near the gate, a drinking trough commemorates the tragic death of Ellen Acland, Sir Francis's ten-year-old daughter, who was killed in a bicycle accident on this spot in 1924.

THE WOODLAND

The woods cover more than 480 hectares (1,200 acres) and are almost all freely accessible to visitors, with well-marked paths, some of which are signposted. They have always been important to the estate, providing timber for building repairs, and adding greatly to the landscape. Each area has a character of its own.

Danes Wood and Columb John Wood were planted or replanted principally for their landscape value, the former as an addition to the view from Killerton House, and the latter as a natural extension of the park. Both are full of bluebells, and are particularly beautiful in May and June. White

Granny Baker, who lived in the lodge rent-free in return for opening the gates

Down, Paradise Copse and Ashclyst Forest have a wilder character. These stand on ground which was considered too poor for profitable farming in the early nineteenth century, when they were planted (though the existence of old hedge-banks in the woods shows that cultivation took place), and they were valued primarily for their timber. More recently, thanks to careful management, Ashclyst has become an important site for butter-flies. Fine trees, of many species and at all stages of growth, can be enjoyed within a comparatively small compass, and these woods have an air of remoteness quite out of proportion to their real distance from civilisation. They are splendid places for walkers and naturalists. Sir Francis Acland was a keen practical forester and a founder-member of the Forestry Commission.

A walks leaflet is available.

THE ESTATE

Killerton House and Garden are part of a working agricultural estate which covers ten square miles of the surrounding countryside and includes the village of Broadclyst. There are 240 cottages, and more than 20 farms varying in size from 20 to nearly 200 hectares (49 to 494 acres). Several are open-hall buildings which date back to the late medieval period (fifteenth and early sixteenth centuries), and show evidence of the time when people were living in single-storey houses and cooking on an open hearth, the smoke drifting out through the thatched roof. They have survived because their owners either did not want, or could not afford, to rebuild, and so in the seventeenth century chimneys and first floors with bedrooms were inserted. In the nineteenth century, passages on the first floor gave privacy to the occupants of these bedrooms, and in the twentieth, bathrooms gave added comfort.

The Acland family have been part of this tradition for four centuries, particularly the Great

Sir Thomas, who grew up in a thatched and lattice-windowed house at Holnicote in the late eighteenth century and learnt to love the vernacular traditions so apparent on his many estates. Until the mid-nineteenth century nearly all the buildings on the estate were of cob and thatch construction. The houses were rendered and limewashed, but the red colour of the subsoil can be clearly seen in the cob of farm outbuildings and garden walls.

The increased agricultural knowledge of the nineteenth century is reflected in the many new farm buildings provided by the Great Sir Thomas. These include the farmstead at Newlands, which was planned to set an example of good design for future farm buildings. Other farms, so important in the landscape of the estate, have grown gradually. Newhall and Beare are two examples of farmsteads that have developed from the seventeenth to the twentieth centuries, the earlier buildings being the threshing barns and stock linhays (sheds).

Towards the end of the nineteenth century new farm cottages were erected on many farms by the 11th Baronet. These were of brick and tile construction, and show a sequence of social development from a single ground-floor room to the two-roomed cottage with 'kitchen' and 'best kitchen' (agricultural workers did not have a sitting-room).

The cost of maintaining an estate of this size has always been high. In 1848 the sum entered in the Killerton estate ledger for cottage repairs was £161 4s 6d, and by 1887 this figure had risen to £690 4s 9d. In 1924, finances were still a cause for concern, as Eleanor, Lady Acland explained to her son, Richard: 'Living at Killerton does leave us actually always short of cash. And this year we have had to fork out £200 for C[ubby]'s illness, £180 for electric light, £300 for alterations, £325 for the car.'

Today, the buildings on the estate are maintained using traditional techniques, many painted with Killerton's famous yellow limewash.

MARKER'S COTTAGE, BROADCLYST

Marker's Cottage is an outstanding example of a late medieval house on the Killerton Estate. It takes its name from Sarah Marker, who owned it between 1790 and 1814, but it was probably built in the fifteenth century. Its smoke-blackened thatch and roof timbers result from the open fire it once had in the central hall. Other early features are the window in the lower room, which has never been glazed, and the plank-and-muntin screen with its shoulder-heavy doorway, between the hall and inner room or parlour. Early seventeenth-century features include the fireplace and beam in the hall, stair turret with mullion window and the pargetting in a niche in the hall chambers.

The paintings on the oak screen, however, are the chief glory of the cottage. These include decorative 'grotesque' work, including a cherub, and in contrast a depiction of St Andrew and his cross, set in a landscape with a church and hunting scene, on the fourth panel. The paintings were probably done a hundred years after the house was built, perhaps around 1530–50, and the paint layers confirm that they are all contemporary.

Marker's Cottage is open to the public on three afternoons a week.

Marker's Cottage, Broadclyst

HISTORY OF KILLERTON

by the late Anne Acland

THE EARLY OWNERS

In the sixteenth century Edward Drewe, a successful Elizabethan lawyer, married into the Kildrington family, which had probably been living at Killerton ever since the name was first recorded in 1242. Drewe took possession of the manor and built himself 'a mansion for his own residence', in which he lived until the end of the century, when, having become the Recorder and Member of Parliament for Exeter, he moved away to Broadhembury near Honiton. Killerton was bought in the early seventeenth century by John Acland, the owner of the adjoining manor of Columb John, and the amalgamation of these two properties formed the nucleus of the future Killerton Estate.

The Aclands had risen from small beginnings by sheer genetic luck. Since they were first recorded in 1155 as small freeholders at Acland Barton near Landkey in North Devon, they had never failed to produce at least one male heir in every generation and often many more, so that they had been able to marry heiresses and steadily increase their property. In Elizabeth I's reign an enterprising younger son, John, left home in search of richer land and a milder climate, and bought Columb John, where he prospered so well that in due course this place became the main family seat in preference to Acland Barton. John Acland was prominent in the county as sheriff, Justice of the Peace, Member of Parliament and noted benefactor to the poor; he was knighted by James I and he paid for the armour-clad effigy in his parish church of Broadclyst, not far from that of his predecessor at Killerton, Edward Drewe, who lies there also, dressed in his legal robes.

THE SEVENTEENTH CENTURY

When the Civil War broke out in 1642, a second John Acland was living at Columb John, and he immediately declared himself a strong Royalist and garrisoned his house for the King, winning it a special mention in Clarendon's famous *History* as the only Royalist stronghold near Exeter, when 'that rich and pleasant city' was in Parliamentarian hands. For this, and probably for a contribution to the royal coffers as well, Charles I rewarded him with a baronetcy in 1644. Later, when the fortunes of war were reversed, and Cromwell and Fairfax came down to the west at the head of the New Model Army, the two great generals themselves quartered at Columb John and, according to the Lady Acland of the day, conducted themselves with consideration and kindness. Unfortunately, the same could not be said about the local Parliamentarians of Exeter; after the fighting was over, they avenged themselves by exacting such a heavy fine from Acland that most of his property had to be forfeited or mortgaged, and he came close to ruin.

Sir John Acland bought the Killerton estate in the early seventeenth century. His tomb monument is in Broadclyst church

Sir Hugh Acland, 5th Bt, who rebuilt Killerton House in 1680

entrance archway remained to mark – as they still do – the place which had once seen active service in the Civil War.

THE EIGHTEENTH CENTURY

The eighteenth century saw Killerton transformed. Two splendid marriages brought the Aclands into the front rank of West Country landowners: in 1721 Sir Hugh Acland, 6th Bt (1697–1728), married Cecily Wroth, the heiress to Petherton Park near Bridgwater, and to a handsome fortune besides. In 1745 his son Sir Thomas Acland, 7th Bt (1722–85), repeated the pattern by marrying Elizabeth Dyke, whose dowry included the three large Somerset estates of Pixton near Dulverton, Tetton near Taunton, and Holnicote near Minehead: in token of this brilliant match her surname was added to her husband's and it has remained in use by the main line of the family ever since.

In addition, the epidemics of plague, which every-where followed the war, accounted within six years for the death of Sir John and his next three heirs. Even then the line did not fail, and in 1655 the fourth son, Hugh, became the 5th Baronet. The Aclands' ample supply of sons had never stood them in better stead.

Sir Hugh Acland, 5th Bt (c.1639–1714), was a stabilising figure at a critical time. His marriage to Anne Daniel, the daughter of a wealthy Yorkshire knight, brought him a substantial dowry which he used to such good effect that by the end of the century the Acland estates were freed from debt, the letters-patent of the baronetcy (lost in the 'Troubles') had been renewed, and the family was well on the way back to prosperity. Sir Hugh decided to move over to Killerton, previously used as a dower-house, but a stone marked '1680' near the present front door is the only indication that he ever did anything to alter the Elizabethan building. Columb John fell into disuse, and the house was eventually taken down. Only the chapel and the

Sir Hugh Acland, 6th Bt, whose marriage in 1721 to Cecily Wroth increased the wealth of the family

Sir Thomas Dyke Acland, as he now became, was especially delighted with his new Exmoor properties of Holnicote and Pixton, which between them contained some of the best stag-hunting country in the kingdom; for a time sport took precedence over all other activities. He became an enthusiastic Master of Staghounds, hunting his pack from one end of the moor to the other, and at the end of the day keeping open house for all his friends: stories were told of 70-mile runs, with 500 horsemen in the field, and of splendid feasts at Holnicote and Pixton, where great companies would gather to dine off haunches of venison and drink the stag's health with a quart of claret apiece.

This pattern changed in 1770, when Acland's elder son John married Lady Harriet Fox-Strangways, daughter of the 1st Earl of Ilchester. Sir Thomas then settled Tetton, Pixton and Petherton Park on the young couple, and for the first time gave his own full attention to Killerton. He was by no means satisfied with it as a gentleman's seat. The H-shaped Elizabethan house, with its formal garden, seemed old-fashioned beside the grand classical mansions standing in landscape parks which his friends – such as John Parker at Saltram – were building for themselves; he determined to follow suit and, as a first step, he engaged John Veitch, a young Scottish gardener working for a London nurseryman, to 'lay out a park'. Veitch, who was one day to make his name famous among gardeners, was then a youth of less than twenty who had walked down from Edinburgh to seek his fortune with nothing but ten shillings and his father's blessing. How Sir Thomas came to hear about him is a mystery, but it soon became clear that he had made a lucky choice, for the young man showed an uncommon aptitude for landscape design. He saw at once that Killerton's great charm lay in the contrast between the peaceful slope of the land in front of the house and the volcanic upthrust of the hill behind it, and he concentrated on enhancing, rather than formalising, the landscape. About 500 acres (202 hectares) were enclosed to form the new park, sharply defined by the River Culm on the north and west, and melting imperceptibly into farmland on the south; to the east, the main Exeter-Tiverton road was diverted by Sir Thomas to set

Sir Thomas Acland, 7th Bt, who rebuilt the house in 1778–9; painted in hunting clothes by Joshua Reynolds (Drawing Room)

it further away from the house. The hill itself was richly planted with trees so as to emphasise its height, and to frame the views from the top: there are fine old trees standing on Killerton Clump today which were planted by Veitch in the 1770s.

The siting of a new house was a matter for consideration. Sir Thomas, who at 56 was at the height of his powers and prosperity, liked the idea of a commanding position high on the hill in preference to the old sheltered site, and in 1775 he commissioned the fashionable architect James Wyatt to design him a suitable house. Wyatt produced drawings of a grand mansion in the classical style, 153 feet (47m) long, with impressive porticos at the front and back; such a large building could only have been sited on the great level stretch of ground at the back of the Clump known as 'the Plain of the Park', where it would certainly have looked remarkably well. However, there were difficulties and hesitations in the architect-client relationship, and it was three years before the contract drawings were signed on 14 April 1778. By that time, Sir Thomas had decided to put up a temporary house on the old site as a stop-gap, and he engaged another, less fashionable, architect, John Johnson, who was so quick to act that by July the builder was taking measurements and by September new walls were rising on the site of Drewe's old house. In the end, Wyatt's palace on the hill was never built. John Acland – newly returned from America with his wife Harriet after brave exploits in the War there, which added a strange romantic chapter to the family record (see p. 00) – died in November, as the result of a duel, and his father had no heart for more grand schemes at Killerton. Johnson's 'temporary' house remained for good.

John Johnson (1732–1814) is best remembered for his civic buildings in Essex, where he later became county surveyor, but at this stage he was chiefly employed in London property development, with an occasional commission for a country house. His reputation for being 'exceedingly honest, cheap and ingenious' would certainly have appealed to Sir Thomas after all Wyatt's delays. The contract ran very smoothly. As the new house was more or less in the same position as the old, some of the foundations could be used again (a great saving of time and money), and by November the ground

floor was so well advanced that William Spring the builder reported that 'the three Mahogany Doors' had gone up in the Great Parlour; by April the carpenters had finished work on the 'Chamber Floor above stairs', and by May the paper-hangers were in. The house was ready by June 1779, less than a year after building had begun. Killerton House has been so much altered and extended by subsequent generations that it is necessary to go round to the south side – Johnson's original front door – to appreciate his design. The fine recessed stone doorway, with its classical pediment and columns, can then be seen as the main entrance to the house which Johnson intended it to be. It is the central feature of an otherwise plain, well-proportioned rectangular building; 'a very neat white mansion' in the eyes of a contemporary topographer. The architect's true talent is shown to much better advantage in the stable block at the bottom of the drive, which was completed a year later than the house. Here, there is no hint of economical or temporary construction. The walls of dressed Killerton stone, the handsome painted cornice, the impressive pedimented archway and the elegant cupola all suggest that Sir Thomas (who had been a keen owner of racehorses for some years) had instructed his architect to spare no

John Johnson's south front with his original front door

Sir Thomas Acland, 9th Bt, returning from a hunt on his Holnicote estate, where he spent most of his life; painted by Francis Towne (Staircase)

expense, and this delightful building is Johnson's best memorial at Killerton.

Meanwhile, John Veitch had won his master's confidence to such an extent that – young as he was – Sir Thomas had set him up in business as an independent nurseryman, on land at Budlake near Killerton, and had also made him agent for all the Acland estates. This soon entailed heavy responsibility, for in 1785 Sir Thomas died. The next (8th) Baronet died as a child; while the 9th Baronet cared for nothing but hunting and seldom came to Devon. During all this interregnum of 23 years Veitch managed the estate single-handed, under Weech the family lawyer. It was not until 1808, when another Sir Thomas, the grandson of his old master, reached his majority that Killerton came to life again.

THE NINETEENTH CENTURY

The nineteenth century was the golden age of Killerton. Under the patriarchal rule of Sir Thomas Acland, 10th Bt (1787–1871), and his wife Lydia, the house took on new life, both as a family home and as a centre of political and philanthropic activity, while the garden grew into full maturity with the continuing help of John Veitch and his descendants. 'The Great Sir Thomas', as he is called within the family, was left fatherless at the age of eight, and he was strictly brought up at Holnicote by his masterful mother Henrietta and her second husband, Matthew Fortescue, on principles very different from those of his father and grandfather. Just as they had been typical of the carefree sporting squires of eighteenth-century England, so did young Acland reflect the more serious mood of his own time. The vigour and spirit which they had thrown into stag-hunting he poured into public work, with a rare moral courage which enabled him

Henrietta Acland, who dominated the childhood of her son, Sir Thomas Dyke Acland, 10th Bt; painted about 1795 (Music Room)

to take an independent line regardless of his own interests. In this spirit, he voted for Catholic Emancipation, Parliamentary reform and the repeal of the Corn Laws, all in the face of opposition from his friends and colleagues – and, though he was in Parliament for a total of 40 years, his fellow Tories never considered him to be 'a quite satisfactory party man'. Apart from the welfare of his estates, education and religion were his two main interests, travel and sketching his chief recreations, and he was blessed with vigorous good health which enabled him to enter with gusto into everything he did.

His wife Lydia, a member of the Hoare banking family, came from Mitcham in Surrey, where she had been brought up in close contact with the austere Evangelical circle which, under William Wilberforce, fought for the abolition of the Slave Trade. She combined a handsome presence with a strong personality and considerable musical talent; she also possessed a constitution of iron. She bore her husband ten children in eighteen years and yet always managed to accompany him wherever his impulsive temperament took him – whether to London for the Parliamentary session, to Vienna for the 1814 Congress, or to Rome in the family yacht, *The Lady of St Kilda*. Even in an age when much was expected of wives, Lydia was an outstanding figure.

When young Sir Thomas first brought his bride to Killerton in 1808 ('we came in our own carriage with four horses and we were young people and we enjoyed it!'), he found the house refurbished from top to bottom after its long period of disuse. His mother Henrietta had been busy for months, making arrangements with builders, and ordering wallpaper, carpets and a complete new set of furniture from Carter the Exeter cabinetmaker. Not even the dinner service ('a great bargain!') was left for Tom and Lydia to choose, and they must have been glad to find that there was still plenty to be decided in the garden. Here, they had an excellent adviser in John Veitch, who was now a man of 56 with a reputation as a nurseryman and a landscape designer which had spread far beyond Killerton. His original planting in the park was coming to splendid maturity, but the deer grazed close up to the house and the only sign of a garden was a modest railed-off area on one side of the entrance. Lydia wanted something more like the garden at her home, Mitcham Grove, where there were lawns, wide gravel walks, a shrubbery and a thatched summer-house as well as many fine trees. Veitch was eager to respond. A substantial part of the park was immediately fenced off against the deer, and laid out as a landscaped garden; before the end of the year he was reporting:

The Ground is planted and the walks formed and all the Turf laid.... The Shrubbery part is also planted with laurels and the best kind of Hardy Shrubs, and only a few tender ones as also the edges of the Shrubbery with Perennial flower roots which I got from Lord Eliot's Garden and some the Gardener got from other Gardens in the neighbourhood. But I think to leave the Gravelling the walks ... as the Expense of drawing the Gravel is very heavy, particularly in wet

The 'Great Sir Thomas': Sir Thomas Dyke Acland, 10th Bt, on the election hustings at Exeter; painted by William Owen in 1818 (Staircase)

Lydia, Lady Acland with her sons Thomas and Arthur; painted by Sir Thomas Lawrence in 1814–15 (Music Room)

weather.... I have also brought forward the Corner of the Rookery Wood where the walk comes out, with large Beech Trees for a Beech Grove finishing at the Large Cedar Tree on the side of the Hill.

Veitch went on to outline plans for a new sunk deer-fence, a mile long, and concluded, 'I shall take care when the Ice comes to get some in as the Ice-House is finished at last'. The Ice-House can still be seen, built into the back of the rock garden (then only a quarry), and large enough to hold 40 tons of ice. Luckily, the ponds froze hard that winter, and 30 men were employed for five days, filling the Ice-House to capacity; this was enough, thought Veitch, for two or three years' supply. It never troubled Sir Thomas that his improvements usually cost far more than he expected, for he was open-handed to a fault – quite as ready to spend £500 on a new school for Broadclyst as find £400 for his own park fence – and his name headed the subscription lists of many good causes in Devon.

In 1812, at the age of 25, he became one of Devon's two Tory MPs, and entered upon a long political career which was notable for its integrity. The short Parliamentary sessions of the day (six

The orangery, as illustrated in John Gendall's Fragments of Killerton *(1831). It was demolished in the late 1930s*

months at the most) left plenty of time for country landowners to spend on their estates; Sir Thomas and his wife usually took a house in London from February until July, and divided the rest of the year between Killerton and Holnicote, with occasional visits to Cornwall, where properties at Bude and Trerice (near Newquay) had now been added to the Acland empire. Killerton, as the principal estate, was much improved during the next two decades as the Great Sir Thomas grew to his full stature as a Parliamentarian and a county magnate. The house was extended back into the hill, to accommodate an increasing number of children, and the dining-room (the present Music Room) was almost doubled in size by the addition of a bow-fronted projection facing east. The park and garden were likewise much elaborated, and Killerton began to appear in the topographical prints of the day as a 'gentleman's seat'. In 1831 Sir Thomas commissioned John Gendall to make a set of pencil drawings, and the resulting album, *Fragments of Killerton*, shows how much Veitch and his employers had achieved by that date. Among the scenes which are clearly recognisable are the Beech Walk – already well established – and the little summer-house now known as the 'Bear's Hut' (after a famous family pet), which is still one of the garden's most popular attractions. It was built for Lydia, who loved her garden as much as her music, and she called it 'Lady Cot'. With its lattice windows, ceiling of matting and pine-cones, 'hermit's chamber' complete with stained-glass window, and floor made from deers' knuckle-bones, it was just such a rustic hut as Jane Loudon described in her book *Gardening for Ladies* (1846), and we may be sure that Lydia spent some happy hours there. Unfortunately, a handsome orangery for tender plants, which Gendall showed standing alongside the main gravel walk, was demolished in the late 1930s.

The album includes a drawing of Columb John chapel, showing it much overgrown with ivy, and wearing an air of neglect. The Killerton party still went across on Sundays to hear the service read by the family chaplain, but it was a long walk and the little building could seat only a dozen people. 'That Pillar of the Church in Devonshire' (as Dean Stanley of Westminster called Sir Thomas) needed a

domestic chapel nearer home, which would be large enough to hold his full retinue of servants, estate workmen and farm tenants; in 1837, therefore, he commissioned the distinguished architect C. R. Cockerell with instructions to copy the chapel of St Joseph at Glastonbury – a Norman ruin which had taken his fancy. Cockerell was best known for his classical designs, but he agreed, and after many delays (and an unexpectedly high final account) the new Killerton chapel was consecrated on 21 September 1841; here, until the end of his days, Sir Thomas would come on Sunday mornings

The chamber organ was installed in the Music Room in 1807 for Lydia, Lady Acland

to join in the very plain service, shaking hands afterwards and marking down absentees with an eagle eye 'like the veteran father of a very large family'.

Killerton was full of life during the long Parliamentary recess. Two sons of the family were already married (Thomas, the eldest, being now MP for West Somerset); another was training to be a doctor, and a fourth was preparing for ordination. They all came frequently to Killerton, where the home party still included two daughters and a schoolboy son. In addition, there was a constant stream of visitors: Acland, Hoare, Fortescue and Herbert relations; county neighbours like the Cliffords, Courtenays, Northcotes, Coleridges and Kennaways; friends from further afield, such as J. S. Harford of Blaise Castle, near Bristol, and 'Chevalier' Bunsen, the Prussian ambassador. Samuel Cousins, the engraver, was often in the house, copying the family portraits, and Samuel Sebastian Wesley (then the organist at Exeter Cathedral) came regularly to give Lady Acland lessons on her own organ. The new dining-room often held parties of eighteen or twenty guests, and there must have been many people who, as the Bishop of New Jersey wrote to his hostess, cherished memories of 'Killerton and of the Sweet days spent there'.

The garden now took on a new and unexpected interest. John Veitch had died at the age of 87, but his nursery business flourished in Exeter under his son James, who inaugurated the policy of sending plant-hunters to remote parts of the world: this eventually made the firm famous, and William Lobb, who travelled to America in 1840, was the first of many. Sir Thomas benefited greatly from these expeditions, for the sheltered position and lime-free soil of Killerton made an ideal trial-ground for most of the new discoveries. His customary Sunday walk round the garden held new excitement when he could watch, inch by inch, the growth of plants which had never before been seen in England, and he could point out with pride to his friends such novelties as the Californian Giant Redwood, which had been raised from the first packet of seed ever to be sent back to this country. Many trees and shrubs still flourishing at Killerton can claim the same distinction.

Until his wife died in 1856, Sir Thomas continued to be an active Member of Parliament, and he found himself moving steadily towards the progressive, or 'Peelite', side of his party. He never described himself as anything other than a Tory, but many of his views were truly liberal, and his speeches and votes were invariably in support of the 'underdog' – whether that underdog was an African slave or a North-Country mill worker. At the outset of his career, Sir Thomas had helped to found the famous Grillion's dining club for MPs of opposite opinions, and he was still one of the club's most respected members when it celebrated its Jubilee in 1863: this was a measure of his lifelong tolerance. He died in 1871 at the age of 84, and he was buried beside his wife at Columb John, where a massive patriarchal tombstone records their ten children and 37 grandchildren. Many memorials in different places were erected for the Great Sir Thomas, but he would have liked none of them better than the granite cross, bearing the names of 40 friends,

Sir Thomas Acland, 11th Bt, modernised the family estates; plaster relief in the Music Room

which stands on the western edge of the beautiful garden which he had done so much to create.

The new Sir Thomas was a man of 62 when he became the 11th Baronet. A wonderfully happy second marriage had helped him to overcome the tragedy of being early widowed, which had left him with five young children, and he had brought up his family at Sprydon, a house a mile away from Killerton which his father had acquired for the purpose. Possessing his full share of what has been called 'the uncomfortable Acland conscience', he had sacrificed a promising political career by voting for the repeal of the Corn Laws in 1846, thereby disgusting many of his supporters and putting himself out of Parliament for twenty years. His pioneer work for education and agriculture (he had transformed the moribund Bath and West Society into a live educational force, and had inaugurated the Local Examination system) might well have earned him office in Gladstone's government if it had not been for this long period in the political wilderness. As it was, he sat as a Liberal backbencher, content to know that his opinion on his own special subjects was always sought. With his thorough knowledge of modern agriculture and his good business sense (something which had been denied to previous generations), 'Thomas the Eleventh' made an excellent landlord. His great object was to put the family estates into first-class order after his father's long rule of almost careless benevolence, and in his 27 years of ownership he achieved it by a policy of frugal living, personally supervised management, and avoidance of expenditure on anything which he considered an extravagance, the two prime examples of this being the garden and the deer in the park. His friend, Lord Portsmouth, persuaded him to keep the deer ('I find nothing so pacific as venison'), but the garden was left to grow by itself. Grandchildren and their cousins thoroughly enjoyed a place where they could lose themselves in the bushes and pull down scarlet creepers to decorate the dining-room table without fear or rebuke; but there was no doubt that when Sir Thomas the Eleventh died in 1898, Killerton Garden was in need of a thorough review.

THE EDWARDIANS

Sir Charles Thomas Dyke Acland, 12th Bt (1842–1919), had all his father's good qualities as a landowner. He carried out his public duties with great diligence, but his main concern was always for his estates: as his brother Arthur said, 'Charlie's mind was essentially feudal'. He and his wife Gertrude were typically Edwardian, both in appearance and in manners. He was stocky but dignified, with a majestic beard; she was tall, graceful and always perfectly dressed. Both of them had a taste for formality and grandeur which was something new to Killerton. Their great tragedy was that they had no children. Perhaps this made Charlie all the more determined to make his mark, for within three months of his father's death he had embarked upon a costly programme of alterations which thoroughly changed the character of Killerton.

Country-house fashions of the day demanded space in which to entertain large house parties.

Sir Charles Acland, 12th Bt, added the single-storey extension which includes the Study; painted by Hubert von Herkomer (Drawing Room)

43

Charlie and Gertie considered it necessary to have a billiard-room, a grand drawing-room and a living-hall opening off the main staircase, where assembled guests could watch the ladies sweeping down to dinner in their evening gowns. To provide all these things at Killerton required a drastic reorganisation of the ground floor; this was achieved by removing important structural walls, building a new staircase and shifting the front door round to the east of the building – the side on which the visitor approaches the house today. The top of the drive was re-designed to make an ample gravelled sweep for visiting carriages, with a new entrance porch (since demolished) and Charlie's single-storey billiard-room on the far side. A scheme for an elaborate wrought-iron archway, incorporating the family arms and high enough to accommodate a tall lady wearing a hat on top of an omnibus ('not at all an unlikely equipage to arrive', thought Charlie), was fortunately abandoned on grounds of cost; even so, the final account for all the new improvements

came to £8,000, at a time when a new pair of brick-built cottages cost £400 and a good housemaid could be got for £12 a year. 'It was all very unlike the Aclands!' as one relation observed. Neverthe-less, most of the visitors appreciated the grandeur of Gertie's new drawing-room with its scagliola pillars, the great oak staircase descending into the hall, and the novel comforts of electric light, central heating and up-to-date sanitation, while the gentle-men particularly enjoyed the luxury of a billiard-room where they were allowed to smoke, instead of being sent out of doors to the orangery.

The garden demanded much attention after its years of neglect: according to John Coutts, the new head gardener, 'All the ground above the beech-walk was a thicket of laurels 40 and 50 feet high', and semi-wild rhododendrons straggled all over the lawns, choking the choicer plants. Gertrude was a great lover of gardening in the naturalistic style of Gertrude Jekyll and William Robinson, and it was Robinson himself whom she called in to give advice on Killerton. He recommended a drastic clearance of all overgrown common stuff, 'effective groups' of new trees and shrubs, and a broad herbaceous border at the bottom of the slope. He also designed a long terrace wall to divide the garden from the park, which was not an unqualified success. According to Coutts, friends chaffed Charlie and Gertie unmercifully about 'that terrible terrace', but at the great silver wedding party which took place in 1905 the guests could not help admiring the greatly improved look of the garden, as they walked over smooth lawns, now cleared of bushes, and looked up at 'Lady Gertrude's Glade' of rhododendrons among the Giant Redwood trees at the top of the slope. Very soon, an elaborate rock garden was made out of the old quarry behind the Bear's Hut – leaving in place the fragment of the Giant's Causeway which stood there as a trophy from the Great Sir Thomas's travels. Many new magnolias, azaleas and other rare plants were added to the grounds, for the Veitch family continued to send out their travellers to distant lands, and Killerton remained a favourite trial-ground. In 1909, Coutts went to Kew, where he later became the curator, handing over the garden to a fellow Scot, John Wilson. 'You will find her Ladyship very keen', he wrote to his successor. Keen she continued to be, as long as her health would allow, but alas it failed prematurely, and by the time the First World War came in 1914 she was able to enjoy her beloved garden only from an invalid carriage.

Charlie died in 1919, a staunch traditionalist to the last. Not until the end of his life did he show much sign of the family's progressive spirit, but two years before the end of the war he created a sensation by handing over to the National Trust 8,000 acres of his Exmoor land on a 500-year lease, thereby more than doubling the land under the Trust's control, anticipating by twenty years its 'covenanting' scheme which is so popular today, and foreshadowing his great-nephew Richard's outright gift of the Killerton and Holnicote estates to the nation in 1944. It was a paradoxical act for the last Edwardian to make and it is his best memorial.

BETWEEN THE WARS

As Charlie had no son to succeed him, the title went to his brother Arthur, now a man of 72 with a distinguished career in education and politics behind him. Arthur had no wish to take on the duties of a country squire and he immediately handed over the management of the family estates to his son Francis – eventually the 14th Baronet. At 47, Francis was himself a Liberal statesman of repute, having held office on the fringe of Asquith's wartime Cabinet, and his wife Eleanor Cropper was as keen a politician as he was; between them they personified the wave of Liberalism which had swept the country in 1906 and which was still strong in the west of England. With their family of four lively children they brought a warmth and vitality to Killerton which had long been lacking: in direct contrast to Charlie's stiff Edwardian style, their way of living was unconventional and openly political: young people's dances and Liberal socials were held in Gertie's grand drawing-room; the billiard-table was shifted so that the boys could carpenter and make canoes, and the processions up and down the great oak staircase were of children and unruly spaniels instead of the stately ladies for whom it had been designed. These were the days when talk of politics dominated every meal, when Francis fought four elections within three years in his home constituency of Tiverton (twice with success), and when a younger son jokingly announced his intention of advertising for refuge in a 'quiet Conservative household': the crowning event of the period was the visit of Lloyd George in 1926, when he launched his new Land Policy from the 'terrible terrace' to a rally of 19,000 people in the park below. No wonder that enthusiastic supporters spoke of Killerton as 'the Castle Beautiful of Liberalism!'

At about this time, a disastrous fire forced Francis to undertake massive reconstruction work at the back of the house, and he took the opportunity of getting rid of Charlie's awkward porch, and building a new entrance hall. The old inner hall then took on a new lease of life as the centre of all sorts of family activities. It was renamed the Music Room and it often lived up to its name, for Eleanor

Acland was one of four musical sisters, and she played the piano very well herself: music, often on two pianos, was a regular part of Killerton evenings when the house was full. As for Francis, his great hobby was the garden. He had a passionate love of rhododendrons and he was especially interested in the many new species which Frank Kingdon-Ward was then discovering in western China. He subscribed to Kingdon-Ward's expeditions, and in return got packets of seed which he raised with an enthusiasm worthy of his great-grandfather, himself driving in bamboo canes to make sure of the best positions and eagerly awaiting the first flowering of the young plants: there was usually a vase full of some rare sort in the Music Room when Francis was at home. His excellent eye for garden design was used to great effect in 1930, when a great gale blew down twenty huge old trees on the lawn below the Bear's Hut, and he was forced to replant the whole of the area.

It was a terrible blow to the family when Eleanor died unexpectedly in 1933, still in the full vigour of her public work for the local community and for the Liberal Party. Francis survived her for six years, driving himself hard at work in Parliament and also in Devon, where he was an outstandingly progressive chairman of the County Council's education committee. In 1935, Richard, his eldest son, was elected Liberal MP for North Devon and in the following year he married Anne Alford, the writer of this guidebook.

It is as a visiting daughter-in-law that I remember Killerton in those last few years before the Second World War. Much of the conversation between Richard and his father was about the League of Nations, and political pamphlets littered the house. Both men frequently went off to public meetings in their constituencies, returning late to find supper congealing in the huge stone-floored kitchen full of black beetles – Francis having perhaps come down from Paddington overnight and attended a couple of County Council meetings on the same day. His

(Right) Richard Acland campaigning during the election of 1935, when he became MP for North Devon

Sir Francis Acland, 14th Bt, inspecting fire damage to the east side of the house in 1924

one relaxation seemed to be his love of plants. I well remember how he would walk at speed to the top of the garden before breakfast, even when he had come down on the night train; how he would run back through the garden door to pick a sweet-smelling nosegay for some departing guest, and how he would look forward to Sunday afternoons when the garden was always open to the public. He made a large map, on which were pin-pointed the week's special attractions, and the more people came the better he was pleased. How glad he would be to know that nowadays more than 100,000 people enjoy Killerton every year!

In 1937 Francis made a second marriage to Constance Dudley, a family friend, but less than two years later he died, just as the Second World War was about to begin, leaving Killerton to his son, Richard.

THE NATIONAL TRUST
by Sir John Acland, 16th Bt

The story of the gift of Killerton and Holnicote estates deserves a special place in the National Trust's history, for it is one of unparalleled political motivation.

In 1939, my parents' world was turned upside down. Their idyllic life in a terraced house in London had seemed under no threat. My father, Richard Acland, was a budding 32-year-old Liberal Member of Parliament, although recently and secretly converted to socialism. My mother, Anne, only 25, had just qualified as an architect and was the mother of a baby son. Then came the bomb-shell of Sir Francis Acland's death. Inheriting titles and estates was not only unexpected; it was also unwelcome.

Anne, Lady Acland, who persuaded her husband Richard to give Killerton to the National Trust; pastel by Barbara Campron, 1978 (Entrance Hall)

Yet the war years were perhaps the most productive period of their lives. For my father they meant the chance for a socialist crusade; preaching common ownership and new morality, he founded the Common Wealth Party which won victories in three by-elections. For my mother they meant the chance to establish herself at Killerton, managing the estate in the absence of the agent (who had been called up) and coming to love the community to which she dedicated herself. To get round the estate, she even learned to ride a bicycle – no mean feat in view of the side-effects of childhood polio.

In October 1942, my father returned from London and, in my mother's words, 'sprang the idea' on her that he would 'get rid of the estates', selling all 17,000 acres (6,880 hectares) in order to raise funds for his political party. She retorted that 'the estates are not just property; they are communities of people for whom I feel responsible'. A three-month impasse followed. Finally, they agreed

on a solution: most of the estates would be given to the National Trust, but in order to provide funds for the Common Wealth Party, about 1,500 acres (607 hectares) would be sold to the Trust. My mother wrote that 'this compromise satisfied Richard's scruples about private property and my own concern for the long term well being of the estates'.

The gift was highly controversial and attracted much criticism in the press. Yet my father's only regrets were, in the first place, that no other landowners followed his example and, later, that common ownership never materialised.

For Killerton House, the war was just as much of an upheaval. The family moved out to the dower-house to accommodate two schools, Battle Abbey (girls) and Vine Hall (boys), which were evacuated from Hastings. Even the Bear's Hut was occupied – both as a classroom and as teachers' sleeping quarters. Most of the house furniture was put into store. Unfortunately, this perished in the Exeter blitz; otherwise, Killerton came through the war with very little damage.

After the war, my parents returned to the top rooms which lie against the hill, while the bulk of the building became home first to the Workers Travellers Association and then to St Luke's College students. My father was a lecturer at St Luke's in the early 1960s and he later became Warden at Killerton: a job which took him up to retirement.

In 1977 the family moved to the dower-house for the last time when the northern part of Killerton became the Regional Headquarters of the National Trust. The main rooms were opened to the public the following year. At the same time, the splendid Paulise de Bush Costume Collection was presented to the Trust for display on the first floor.